GRAND HOMES
OF THE
MIDWEST

Text
Bill Harris

Photography
Ric Pattison

Design
Clive Dorman

Editorial
Gill Waugh
Louise Houghton

Production
Ruth Arthur
David Proffit
Sally Connolly

Director of Production
Gerald Hughes

Director of Publishing
David Gibbon

ACKNOWLEDGMENT
The publisher wishes to thank all the individuals and
organizations who so willingly provided assistance, as
well as access to properties, throughout the
preparation and photography for this book. Special thanks
are due to the owners and keepers of the featured homes, and
in particular to the Chicago Architecture Foundation, the David
Davis Museum, the Edsel and Eleanor Ford House, Hearthstone,
Illinois Historic Preservation Agency, Lanier State Historic Site,
Division of Museums and Historic Sites, Indiana Department of
Natural Resources, Tom McGrew, Pabst Mansion, Salisbury
House, Barb Schlueter, Greg Soula, Stan Hywet Hall, The Terrace
Hill Society, Villa Louis, and Leonard W. Weis for supplying
additional help, and photographs.

CLB 2469
© 1990 Colour Library Books Ltd, Godalming, Surrey, England.
All rights reserved.
Color separation by Advanced Laser Graphic Arts (International) Ltd., Hong Kong.
This 1990 edition published by Crescent Books,
distributed by Outlet Book Company, Inc., a Random House Company,
225 Park Avenue South, New York, New York 10003
Printed and bound in Italy.
ISBN 0 517 62376 5
8 7 6 5 4 3 2 1

GRAND HOMES OF THE MIDWEST

Text by
BILL HARRIS

Photography by
RIC PATTISON

CRESCENT BOOKS
NEW YORK

The village of Granville, Ohio, proudly proclaims that it has style with a capital "S", and anyone who visits there not only agrees, but regards the Merchants' Association's boast as an understatement. Its streets are shaded by tall maples and lined with charming nineteenth-century houses and inns. "Virtually a museum of days gone by," claim the Granvilleites. But wait a minute ... this little town at the geographical center of Ohio looks for all the world like what they call a typical New England town up in Massachusetts. It's no coincidence. The majority of the towns in what they called the "Western Reserve" back in the early nineteenth-century were little tintypes of New England villages. Granville came by it honestly because it was settled in 1805 by emigrants from Connecticut and Massachusetts, who quite naturally built their homes to resemble the ones they had left behind. But in those days Boston was the cultural hub of the country, and even migrants into Ohio, Indiana and beyond – who had never ventured anywhere near New England – were influenced by what people were thinking there.

Their ideas in terms of architecture had neither been born in America, nor been introduced here through New England.

Thomas Jefferson had started the ball rolling in the direction of creating a purely American architectural style when he wrote, "As we double our numbers every twenty years, we must double our houses. ... Architecture is among the most important arts; and it is desirable to introduce taste into an art which shows so much." He wasn't all talk either; on returning from his years in France, he was embued with an enthusiasm for the architecture of the noble Romans, and convinced his neighbors that they too could achieve a kind of nobility through classical symmetry.

By the time Americans began moving across the Appalachians, the accent had shifted from Latin to Greek. Not only that, but the style known as Greek Revival had become a national passion. It came to America in the minds of well-trained architects, arriving from Europe in the late eighteenth century in the knowledge that there were commissions aplenty waiting for them.

Chief among them was Benjamin Latrobe. Latrobe had earned a degree in engineering in Germany and had studied architecture in London, where the Greek influence was beginning to merge with the adaptations of Roman splendor that had taken the previous generation of Englishmen by storm. Not long after he arrived in Norfolk in 1796, he attracted Jefferson's attention and through him received a commission to build the Philadelphia Water Works, a massive structure the like of which America had never seen before. Along with his landmark Bank of Pennsylvania, it established him as the country's leading architect. And if Thomas Jefferson didn't agree with his sources, he never said so. Jefferson became Latrobe's patron and, as President in 1804, made the architect the government's official surveyor of public buildings. In this role Latrobe worked closely with William Thornton, the amateur who had won the competition for the design of the Capitol

Building in Washington. In turn Latrobe designed the south wing following Thornton's ideas, which, after all, had followed his own initial vision. By the time Latrobe died in 1820, Greek Revival had become the only choice among builders and homeowners who wanted to make a just-right impression. The style had become a national passion, but nowhere quite as much so as in the Western Reserve; new towns and cities there competed with each other to be known as the Athens of the West. If nothing else, it gave the pioneers a chance to make a statement that was new and allowed them to thumb their noses at the Eastern gentry. Unless they chose to tear down their old houses and start over, which some did, the Eastern gentry were stuck with old-fashioned Georgian architecture.

It was a new statement. Yes, it had its roots in antiquity, but only the influence was Greek. Latrobe himself had said of the Greeks, "Our religion requires a church wholly different from their temples, our legislative assemblies and our courts of justice buildings of entirely different principles from their basilicas, and our amusements could not possibly be performed in their theaters and amphitheaters." Yet it was a powerful influence that still dominates the American Midwest, which was settled at the height of the movement. The statement that was being made went way beyond aesthetics; it was as American as apple pie and as political as a campaign button.

When Andrew Jackson became President in 1829, the cultural revival had reached Greece itself. The art of Ancient Greece was being excavated and trotted off to overseas museums, the English Romantic poets were singing its praises, and writers around the world were finding inspiration in its mythology. More important to the American psyche, however, Greece was seen as the birthplace of the democratic ideals that were re-born in the American Revolution. Jackson's dictum "let the people rule," was seen as the flowering of the democratic principles of Ancient Greece. Jackson himself was impressed by the independence movement taking place in Greece at the time. When the Greeks drove out their Ottoman rulers early in his presidency, Jackson took it as a sign that the middle class had finally earned the right to become the ruling class; not only in America, but in the world as a whole. His fellow Americans couldn't have agreed more, especially those of the Midwest. The outward sign of the peoples' enthusiasm for Jacksonian democracy was a strong pull in the direction of anything Greek. Until then, the movement had been in the hands of the intelligentsia and the upper classes. Now, thanks to Andrew Jackson, it took its place in the hearts of all the people. While the revolutionaries in Europe were showing their support of democratic principles by wearing Phrygian caps, Americans showed theirs in the homes and public buildings they built.

But, ironically, another new movement was afoot that would soon make Greek Revival an old-fashioned idea. When the Greek style became the property of the middle class, the upwardly mobile began looking for new ways to out-do their inferiors. By the time William Henry Harrison, former Governor of the Indiana Territory, was elected to President, people were beginning to wonder if the legacy of ancient Greece was really as all-American as it was cracked up to be. Radicals were beginning to call it pretentious, even tiresome. It was frequently noted that the ancient Greeks were nothing more than pagans and that the United States was a Christian country worthy of better things than paying homage to a dead culture. Nearly everyone who mattered agreed that it was time to create a uniquely American style. For openers, they once again turned to Europe, this time coming up with an enthusiasm for the Gothic. They began reading Walter Scott novels, and found inspiration in John Ruskin's passion for Venice. Hardly a native American idea, but, as its defenders were quick to point out, it was at least Christian. People went out of their way to live in drafty houses that resembled churches. Some even added chapels, which allowed them to do their duty to God without ever leaving home. But, in spite of the variety of ways there were to individualize the style, following yet another set of dogmatic rules gave them little more than a new cookie cutter. Then a few daring architects began ignoring the rules and combining different styles in a single building. At first it was considered a barbaric idea, but, as long as their work was harmonious, they found it to be in demand. By the 1850s, the patchwork theory was being hailed as a purely "American" style. It was dubbed "Picturesque Eclecticism," but most Americans were more comfortable naming it for England's Queen Victoria. The style had its roots in the America of the 1820s and didn't lose popularity until the time of World War I. Queen Victoria herself reigned from 1837 to 1901. But, after all, the Queen stood for progress, and no one saw any irony in the fact that the first truly American contribution to architecture and design should be called "Victorian."

At first the new ideas didn't exactly take the Midwest by storm. For a start, builders there resented the dictates of Eastern big-city architects. When Alexander Jackson Davis, that great proponent of the Gothic style, submitted plans for a multi-towered stone pile on the campus of the University of Michigan, locals were none too impressed. They pointed out that his building was not only extravagantly expensive, but would "require a fortune to provide fuel to keep it comfortably warm in winter." Davis' colleague, Andrew Jackson Downing, who had pioneered naturalistic landscaping and championed "rural" architecture, generally wrote off the Midwest as a wild frontier. "So long as men are forced to dwell in log huts and follow the hunter's life, we must not be surprised at lynch law and bowie knives," he wrote. "But when smiling lawns and tasteful cottages begin to embellish a country, we know that order and culture are established" he continued. Such statements were good for business in the Hudson Valley. However, culture and order had crossed the mountains long before Downing was born, and those folks on the frontier resented any implication that they were little more than uncouth wild men. Still, they did agree that a smiling lawn and a tasteful house could go a long way toward keeping barbarism at bay. So, of course, could an expanding population.

Once the Indian wars were over, settlers from the Northeast flocked westward. Immigrants from Europe didn't even stop for a look around in New York, Boston or Philadelphia, but headed across the mountains to where they were told they'd find *real* opportunity. People came up from the South, too, and in the years between 1810 and 1820, the population of Ohio increased by 152 percent; Illinois by 350 percent, and Indiana by a massive 500 percent. By the 1850s the territory from Ohio to Missouri to Michigan and Wisconsin had all the hallmarks of a genuine melting pot. There was still plenty of land to go around, but by mid-century more Americans lived west of the Alleghenies than in New England and the Northeastern states combined. By the end of the century, the Midwest had given us six out of the seven presidents elected between 1860 and 1900.

During the years of growth land speculators were everywhere, promising unlimited acres of rich, fertile farmland at prices anyone could afford. However, not everyone is cut out to be a farmer. For those who preferred to live in towns, the speculators had even better deals. After all, there's more money to be made in subdivision than in farm acreage, and visions of new towns on the banks of a river or at a crossroads made for some very appealing promotion. It was a game anybody could play, and most did. A foreign tourist noted in his description of Ohio that, "If you accost a farmer in these parts, before he returns your civilities, he draws from his pocket a lithographic city and asks you to take a few building lots at one-half their value as a personal favor conferred on you." Even at half-price it was a profitable enterprise. Government land was selling for two dollars an acre in the early 1800s; each acre committed to a townsite could be divided into a dozen building lots that could go for ten to fifty dollars apiece. Town planners offered easy terms, too. A prospective buyer made a downpayment equal to a quarter of the asking price, with the balance payable in easy instalments over a year – with interest, of course. The only other requirement before a deed would be issued was that the buyer promise to put a building on the lot within two or three months.

The speculators usually promised to give away lots for a courthouse, a school, a tavern and a store, and many actually built them, though never until the majority of building lots were sold. There was no point in throwing good money after bad, after all. Many of the proposed towns never made it off the drawing boards because their promoters had made off with the funds. Others, however, really did make it.

None other than Charles Dickens was said to have been taken in by speculators selling lots in Cairo, Illinois, which today is a charming little city at the point where the Ohio River meets the Mississippi. Whether he actually invested in the town isn't known, but he visited there in 1842 and vented his spleen on the town fathers both in his novel "Martin Chuzzlewit," and in his "American Notes." In the latter he wrote, "We arrived at a spot so much more desolate than any we had yet beheld, that the forlornest places we passed were, in comparison with it, full of interest. ... [it is] a breeding place of fever, ague and death, vaunted in England as a mine of Golden Hope and speculated in, on the faith of monstrous misrepresentations, to many people's ruin ... the hateful Mississippi circling and eddying before it and turning off upon its southern course, a slimy monster hideous to behold; a hotbed of disease, an ugly sepulchre, a grave uncheered by any gleam of promise: a place without one single quality, in earth, air or water, to command it: such is this dismal Cairo."

Well, you can't please everyone. In 1837, a New Englander began building a levee to hold back the "hateful" Mississippi, and his business agents in Chicago went to work to sell building lots behind it. He also hired a London real estate firm to promote the town, but it went bankrupt, leaving its investors high and dry. Then Cairo itself began to dry up. By 1842 its population had dropped to a hundred and the town was deep in debt. It got a new lease on life when a railroad connected it to Chicago, but thanks to its overeager speculators and its bad press from the likes of Charles Dickens, Cairo never did become a major city, in spite of its strategic location.

The towns and cities that did survive, whether due to their location on a canal, river or railroad, or their designation as a county seat, very quickly abandoned the trappings of the frontier in favor of a kind of gentility that is still alive and well in the Midwest. When Booth Tarkington set the stage for *The Magnificent Ambersons* by describing a typical neighborhood in Indianapolis, he could have been writing about any number of towns in the Midwest in the late nineteenth century.

"The houses lacked style," he wrote, "but also lacked pretentiousness, and whatever does not pretend at all has style enough. They stood in commodious yards, well shaded by leftover forest trees, elm and walnut and beech, with here and there a line of tall sycamores where the land has been made by filling bayous from the creek. The house of a 'prominent resident,' facing Military Square or National Avenue or Tennessee Street, was built of brick upon a stone foundation, or of wood upon a brick foundation."

But some residents are more prominent than others, and wealthy merchants and captains of industry, like Tarkington's Major Amberson, improved on the scene with their impressive stone mansions. These had been built in emulation of the robber barons and tycoons back East, who routinely used architecture to call attention to their wealth. Amberson was pleased to boast that he had spent "sixty thousand dollars for the woodwork alone," on his house. The mansions didn't always have the benefit of professional architects, but builders and prospective homeowners found plenty of books and magazines to give them ideas and guide them through the process of creating an impressive house. A man could make just about any statement he cared to when he built his house. As the architectural historian John Maass explained, "Each style contained a distinct 'message.' A Gothic Revival house usually signified that the owner was proud to be of old English stock. An Italianate villa did not mean that the owner was of Italian descent but 'This is a 'cultured and artistic household.' and a French style proclaimed 'This is a stylish and fashionable home.' ... 'Fine men build fine houses' was accepted as a true statement. Hence it was a short step to reversing the proposition: 'If you own a fine house you will be taken for a fine man.' Nineteenth-century America usually equated affluence with virtue."

In the years after the Civil War, affluence, if not virtue, seemed to be the rule of the day. Andrew Carnegie was hauling iron ore across the Great Lakes to build one of the greatest fortunes the country has ever seen. John D. Rockefeller was turning Cleveland into a boom town with his oil refineries, the Pillsburys were revolutionizing the flour business in Minneapolis, and the Armours were building an empire in the Chicago stockyards. The incentive to follow in their footsteps was at its strongest in the Midwest, where the pioneering spirit was still very much alive. By the beginning of the 1890s there were more than 4,000 certified millionaires in America, compared to just a few dozen before the war. Business was booming and that was a heaven-sent opportunity for architects and interior designers to show off their skills. If the country wasn't quite doubling its houses every twenty years any longer, the quantity had been replaced by a demand for quality. Nowhere was the demand for skilled designers greater than in the Midwest, especially Chicago. After the fire that destroyed most of the city in 1871, Chicagoans began rebuilding even before the last embers stopped glowing. The destruction represented an opportunity for architects and builders, but the attitude of the people there made it an extraordinary opportunity, and extraordinary men were on hand to take advantage of it. First among them was Henry Hobson Richardson.

Richardson had made a name for himself back East with his Trinity Church in Boston, among other buildings, but he reached the climax of his career when he arrived in Chicago in 1885 to design a warehouse for Marshall Field. It was to be the beginning of America's single greatest architectural movement, the so-called "Chicago School." The buildings Richardson built in Chicago before he died at the age of forty-eight impressed no one so much as Louis Sullivan, whose own architectural philosophies were finally crystallized by Richardson's influence. Sullivan noticed that Richardson's buildings were "direct, large and simple," which led, quite naturally, to his own philosophy that "form follows function."

When Sullivan arrived in Chicago not long after the Great Fire he felt it to be "magnificent and wild: a crude extravaganza, an intoxicating rawness, a sense of big things to be done." Unlike Richardson, whose massive buildings followed the same general form that is still known as "Richardson Romanesque," Sullivan's nearly 125 buildings have nothing more in common with each other than a stroke of architectural genius. Along with Burnham and Root, who built the world's first skyscraper in Chicago, Sullivan pioneered the design of multistoried buildings. His former apprentice, Frank Lloyd Wright, on the other hand, developed the idea of the Prairie House, whose horizontal plans changed the entire concept of separating indoor spaces from the world outside.

The Chicago School of architects was elbowed aside by more powerful Eastern influences which dictated that the general style of Chicago's 1893 Columbian Exposition should be Beaux Arts, the French-modified version of Greek and Roman themes. In the years that followed, the so-called "City Beautiful" movement began altering the face of every city and small town in America. If Americans got the idea that "this is where I came in," they didn't show it. As far as housing was concerned they were still having a love affair with the "Queen Anne" style, loosely based on English country houses of the early 18th century. The so-called Victorians weren't really interested in innovating. What they wanted more than anything else was a sense of roots, a past they could cling to. If they lived in the place where they were born, chances were good that their parents had moved there from somewhere else. They were looking for a sense of permanence, and it was easiest to establish it in the houses they built. If their houses weren't old, they wanted them to at least look as if they were. If they had a coal furnace in the cellar, they also had fireplaces in every room. Many so called Victorians even went to Europe to find antique paneling, stonework, or even entire rooms to make their new houses feel old and established.

The upper classes clung to another tradition by setting their lavish homes slightly apart from the homes of the masses. This made many Midwestern towns similar, at least in feeling, to those towns that dot the English countryside with smaller homes surrounding a grand manor house; that way there was no mistaking who was in charge.

But at the beginning of the twentieth century, Americans began thinking of the future rather than the past. There were more job choices, trolley lines began connecting towns together and the family car made it possible to achieve more freedom of movement. Houses came equipped with electric lights and central heating, and little by little Americans began asking themselves why they should keep on looking to Europe for their inspiration. After all, they kept reminding each other, this is the greatest, most advanced culture anywhere in the world. Many of them became a bit boorish about it and "boosterism" became a dirty word in many circles. It was an era that inspired Edgar Lee Masters to write his *Spoon River Anthology*, filled with the ghosts of people he had known while growing up in rural Illinois. His conclusion was that the best thing that could happen to any of them was to migrate to the big cities or Europe, and even then their unhappy lives didn't improve, possibly because of their Midwestern backgrounds. His impact upon the image of the American Midwest was almost as depressing as Dickens's condemnation had been. Sherwood Anderson twisted the knife a little more with his novel *Winesburg, Ohio*, in which he pulled back the veil on the sex lives of the people of the small Ohio town he had known as a boy. He said that the roots of most of the problems the Midwest was experiencing could be found in the bedroom, and that proper Victorians weren't really all that proper after all. "Sex was a tremendous force in their lives," he said. "It twisted people, beat upon them, often destroyed their lives." Residents of his hometown of Clyde, Ohio, admitted that they recognized themselves in his book, and responded by burning it. This in turn helped to sell a lot of books, and added another dimension to the general perception of Midwesterners. But the *coup de grace* was administered in 1920 when Sinclair Lewis created the mythical town of Gopher Prairie, Minnesota, patterned after his home town, Sauk Centre, in his novel, *Main Street*. "This is America," he proclaimed, "a town of a few thousand, in a region of wheat and corn and dairies and little groves. ... Its Main Street is the continuation of Main Streets everywhere." But Americans everywhere smirked, and said, "No, just the Midwest." Their smirks turned to self-satisfied guffaws when Lewis introduced them to a philistine named George Babbitt in 1922. It only confirmed what they already believed: that the American Midwest was an intellectually stagnant place. They doggedly refused to accept that he was aiming his barbs in their direction, too.

At the time iconoclasts like Sinclair Lewis were railing against the restrictions and class distinctions of small-town life, the population had already started moving away from the farms and small towns in the direction of the big cities. There were undeniable opportunities for jobs there. But after the Great Depression of the 1930s, when jobs became harder to find, young people began trickling back. No matter what they read, or what urban sophisticates told them about the life they had escaped, there was warmth and security in those small towns. Young people began to champion simple values and old traditions, it became fashionable to wear homespun clothing, sing folk songs and long for the uncomplicated life of past generations. Sinclair Lewis himself took to attacking urban intellectualism, and though they agreed with Thomas Wolfe that "You Can't Go Home Again," the young were willing to give it a try. The world was too much with them, and they found solace in the small comforts that had been rejected by the generation that preceded them.

But the towns they came back to had changed, too. The old class structures had broken down for a start. Many of the old elite families had been forced to pare down their lifestyles, and the House on the Hill had even been abandoned in many communities. Even though they had lost standing as symbols of power, they were still symbols of a kind of magnificence. They were also an anchor to that uncomplicated past everyone was longing for, and, fortunately, there was a spirit of preservation abroad in the land.

In earlier times, it had been an American tradition to remove old buildings and replace them with something more in keeping with the current style of life. But in the years between the world wars, attitudes began to change. John D. Rockefeller, Jr. transformed derelict old Williamsburg, Virginia, into a restoration that made it more attractive than at any other time in its history. Henry Ford began buying up historic old homes and moving them to Greenfield Village at Dearborn, Michigan, to surround his own historic birthplace. Eleanor Roosevelt, during her years as First Lady, worked tirelessly to restore the Georgetown section of Washington, D.C., to its former charm. Their enthusiasm was contagious; the results of their work nothing short of inspirational. Soon the idea of reclaiming America's past became a crusade in every part of the country, and the Midwest proved to have more to offer than almost any other region.

But there was also a movement afoot to improve the aesthetic quality and durability of new homes. The basic philosophy on housing architecture had hardly changed in a hundred years, even though those years had seen the advent of electric lights, central heating, and even elevators in our houses. As had happened in the past, the wave of the future was first felt in Chicago, with its second World's Fair – the 1933 Century of Progress. Louis Sullivan had predicted what became an inevitable trend; Frank Lloyd Wright had pushed it along. By 1933, people in Chicago were beginning to agree with Le Corbusier that a house, after all, was nothing more than a machine in which one lived. It was a reiteration of Sullivan's belief that "form follows function."

Inevitably, the Great Depression and World War II put these ideas on the back burner for a while. By the time the war ended young people were beginning to think seriously about their own dream houses. They wanted their homes to incorporate all the modern convenience they had been dreaming about since the 1939 New York World's Fair. As it turned out, their dream houses didn't follow the flat-roofed, modern lines of the houses displayed at the Century of Progress. But if they rejected living in machines, they certainly crammed every nook and cranny of their dormered Cape Cods, sprawling ranches and boxy split-levels with every labor-saving device imaginable. Tradition was hard to deny, but if going "modern" made life easier, well, why not?

But that old tug of the past wouldn't go away. At the beginning of the century, Thomas Hastings, whose New York Public Library and Frick Mansion are landmarks of the "City Beautiful" movement, disaproved of the progression. He lamented that "the medieval mason praised God with every chisel stroke. For him work was worship; and his life was one continuous psalm of praise. Now a Gothic church is built by laborers whose one interest is to increase their wages and diminish their working hours." By mid-century there was a commonly accepted notion that, for all his innovation, Frank Lloyd Wright was never able to solve the problem of leaky roofs. According to popular opinion, the best answer, for those who could afford it, was to buy a nineteenth-century house, built in a time when there were still some craftsmen abroad in the land. But, of course, the interior would have to be modernized. Craftsmanship notwithstanding, a cast iron kitchen sink was no substitute for a dishwasher, and with no servants to help, how could a woman possibly be expected to do the family laundry by hand? It wasn't a perfect solution in the search to make a statement of quality, and predictably there was a better one for the super-rich. If America wasn't producing craftsmen any longer, there were plenty of them in Europe. If work wasn't exactly worship to them, they were still willing to oblige for less. The same sort of propaganda that had tarred Midwesterners with the brush of Babbittry was being used against home-grown builders. "No one does that kind of work anymore. No one cares," was the lament. Captains of industry had been importing stonemasons and plasterers for generations, and though the trend had slowed in the era of income taxes, it was still the very best way to proclaim one's status.

The end result was a mix of building styles as eclectic as the population of America itself. There is something to please just about everyone, and the best part is that Americans have put away the idea of modernizing old homes or tearing them down to follow a new fashion. We have discovered a sense of history and found a commitment to keep the past alive in our historic houses.

Visitors Guide

Most of the homes pictured in these pages may be visited, and many provide guided tours.

Missouri

Chatillon-DeMenil Mansion, 3352 DeMenil Place, St. Louis, Mo. 63118. (314) 771-5828. (pp. 17-21) Mansion and gift shop open Tuesday through Saturday, 10.00 am-4.00 pm. Guided tours available. Restaurant open Tuesday through Saturday, 11:30 am-2.00 pm, reservations advised (314) 771-5829. Admission charged.

The Cupples House, 3673 West Pine Blvd., St. Louis, Mo. 62103. (314) 658-3025. (pp. 22-27) The House and St. Louis University's Art Gallery, located in its former bowling alley, open Monday through Friday, 10.00 am-3.00 pm; Sundays 2.00 pm-4.00 pm. Donation requested.

The Phelps House, 1146 Grand Avenue, Carthage, Mo. 64836. (417) 358-1776. (pp. 28, 29) Open Saturday and Sunday, 2.00 pm-5.00 pm Admission charged.

Garth Woodside Mansion, R.R. #1, Hannibal, Mo. 63401. (314) 221-2789. (pp. 30-33) Operated as a bed and breakfast inn by Irv and Diane Feinberg.

Rockcliffe Mansion, 1000 Bird, Hannibal, Mo. 63401. (314) 21-4140. (pp. 34-37) Guided tours 9.30 am-5.00 pm March through November, 11.30 am-3.30 pm December through February. Admission charged.

Iowa

Terrace Hill, 2300 Grand Avenue, Des Moines, Ia. 50312. (515) 281-3604. (pp. 38, 39) Guided tours of first and second floors and carriage house available Sunday through Thursday, except January and February.

Salisbury House, 4025 Tonawanda Drive, Des Moines, Ia. 50312. (515) 279-9711. (pp. 40, 41) Headquarters of the Iowa State Education Association. Guided tours, Monday through Friday.

Wisconsin

Villa Louis, Box 65, Prairie du Chein, Wi. 53821. (608) 326-2721. (pp. 42-45) Open daily, May through October, 9.00 am-5.00 pm. Tours available. Admission charged.

Wisconsin's Executive Residence, 99 Cambridge Road, Madison, Wi. 53704. (608) 266-3544. (pp. 46-49) Tours available Thursdays, noon-3.00 pm, April through August. Special Christmas open house programs are scheduled in December.

Hearthstone, 625 West Prospect Avenue, Appleton, Wi. 54911. (414) 730-8204. (pp. 50-53) Open Thursdays 10.00 am-noon; Sundays 1.00 am-3.30 pm. Tours available by special arrangement.

Old Wade House Historic Site, Greenbush, Wi. 53026. (414) 526-3271. (pp. 54-57) Open daily May through October, 9.00 am-4.00 pm during July and August and all weekends, 10.00 am-5.00pm. Costumed interpreters invite visitor participation. Admission charged.

Wingspread, Racine, Wi. (pp. 58-63) The H.F. Johnson home is now a conference center operated by the Johnson Foundation. Tours are given of the Johnson Wax Co. World Headquarters, also designed by Frank Lloyd Wright, Tuesday through Friday. They begin at the Guest Relations Center, 14th & Franklin Streets, Racine, Wi. 53401-0547. Reservations are requested. (414) 631-2154.

Captain Frederick Pabst Mansion, 2000 W. Wisconsin Ave., Milwaukee, Wi. 53233-2043. (414) 931-0808. (pp. 64-67) Open daily, March 15-December 31, 10.00 am-3.30 pm, Sundays from noon; January 1-March 14, open weekends only except by appointment. Tours available. Admission charged.

Pierre Menard Home and Fort Kaskaskia, RR 1, Box 63, Ellis Grove, Il. 62241. (618) 859-3741. (pp. 68-71) Open daily 6.00 am-10.00 pm. The park includes picnic areas and campsites.

Ulysses S. Grant Home, 500 Bouthillier St, Galena Il. 61036. (815) 777-0248. (pp. 72, 73) Open daily, except major holidays.

Ronald Reagan Boyhood Home, 816 South Henepin, Dixon, Il. 61021. (pp. 74, 75) Open daily, except Tuesday and major holidays.

Clarke House and Glessner House, 1800 S. Prairie Ave., Chicago, Il. 60616. (312) 326-1393. (pp. 76-85) Tours at noon, 1.00 pm, and 2.00 pm Wednesday, Thursday and Friday, and also at 3.00 pm Saturday and Sunday from April through October; November through March tours are on Wednesday, Friday, Saturday and Sunday, at noon, 1.00 pm and 2.00 pm. Admission charged except Wednesday. The museum houses are operated by the Chicago Architecture Foundation, which offers more than fifty architecture tours annually in the Chicago area and operates ArchiCenter, a gallery and bookstore at 330 S. Dearborn.

David Davis Mansion, 1000 East Monroe Street, Bloomington, Il. 61701. (309) 828-1084. (pp. 86, 87) Open Thursday through Monday 9.00 am-5.00 pm. The last tour begins at 4.00 pm.

Abraham Lincoln Home, 426 S. Seventh St., Springfield, Il. 60703. (217) 492-4150. (pp. 88-91) Open daily.

Indiana

Copshaholm, Oliver House, corner of West Washington and South Chapin streets, South Bend, In. (pp 92-95).

Lanier State Historic Site, 511 West First Street, Madison, In. 47250. (812) 265-3526. (pp. 96-99) Open Wednesday through Saturday 9.00 am-5.00 pm; Tuesday and Sunday from 1.00 pm. Donations welcome.

President Benjamin Harrison Memorial Home, 1230 North Delaware Street, Indianapolis, In. 42606. (317) 631-1898. (pp. 100-103) Open daily except January and major holidays.

Morris Butler House Museum of Mid-Victorian Decorative Arts, 1204 North Park Avenue, Indianapolis, In. 42606. (317) 636-5409. (pp. 104-107) Open Wednesday through Sunday, except major holidays.

William Henry Harrison Mansion (Grouseland), 3 West Scott Street, Vincennes, In. 47591. (812) 882-2096. (pp. 108, 109).

Hillforest, Main Street, Box 221, Aurora, In. 47001. (812) 926-0087. (pp. 110, 111) Open Tuesday through Sunday, 1.00 pm-5.00 pm, May 1 through December 23. Admission charged.

Michigan

Honolulu House, 107 North Kalamazoo Avenue, Marshall, Mi. 49068. (616) 781-4335. (pp. 112-115) Open daily, mid-May through October. The house is headquarters to the Marshall Historical Society, which will guide you to other nineteenth-century buildings nearby.

Meadow Brook Hall, Oakland University, Rochester, Mi. 48063. (313) 370-3140. (pp. 120-125) Tours every Sunday 1.00 pm-5 pm, and Monday through Saturday in July and August. Admission charged. Buffet dinners are served on Sundays and the Summer Tea Room is open weekdays in July and August.

Fair Lane, University of Michigan, Dearborn, Mi. 48128-1491. (313) 593-5590. (pp. 126-129)

Tours every Sunday 1.00 pm-4.30 pm, and Monday through Saturday from April to December. Admission charged. The Pool Restaurant is open all year, Monday through Friday 11.00 am-2.00 pm.

Edsel & Eleanor Ford House, 1100 Lake Shore Road, Grosse Point Shores, Mi. 48236. (313) 884-4222. (pp. 130-135) Tours Wednesday through Sunday on the hour 1.00 pm-4.00 pm.

Ohio

Spiegel Grove, the Hayes Presidential Center, 1337 Hayes Avenue, Fremont, Ohio 43420. (419) 332-2081. (pp. 136-139) Open daily, Presidential Library closed on Sunday.

Lawnfield, James A. Garfield Home, 8095 Mentor Avenue, Mentor, Ohio 44060. (216) 225-8722. (pp. 140-143) Open daily except Monday, May through October. Admission charged.

Stan Hywet Hall and Gardens, 714 North Portage Path, Akron, Ohio 44303. (216) 836-5533. (pp. 144-151) Tours 10.00 am-4.00 pm Tuesday through Saturday, and from 1.00 pm on Sundays. Admission charged. The grounds open at 9.00 am in the summer months. Special events are staged throughout the year, from an Easter egg show in April to madrigal dinners in November and festivities at Christmas.

President Harding Home and Museum, 380 Mt. Vernon Avenue, Marion, Ohio 43302. (614) 387-9630. (pp. 152, 153) Open Wednesday through Sunday from Memorial Day through Labor Day.

Adena State Memorial, Adena Road, Box 831A, Chillicothe, Ohio 45601. (614) 772-1500. (pp. 154, 155) Open Wednesday through Sunday from Memorial Day through Labor Day, and weekends in October. Admission charged.

Robbins Hunter Museum, the Avery Downer House, 221 East Broadway, Box 183, Granville, Ohio 43023. (614) 587-0430. (pp 156-160) Open daily from 1.00 pm-3.30 pm except Monday April through September, and at the same hours on Friday, Saturday and Sunday from October through March. The village of Granville has several other early nineteenth-century buildings, museums and inns.

The Chatillon-DeMenil Mansion (previous page and these pages) was built in downtown St. Louis, Missouri, in 1849. Its Greek-Revival facade was added in 1863. The parlor (facing page top) is named the Chouteau Room for the first white woman to settle in St. Louis. The library (facing page bottom) was originally the back parlor.

Facing page: (top) a bedroom in the Chatillon-DeMenil Mansion (these pages), its original furniture including a half-canopy mahogany bed, and (bottom) the drawing room, furnished in nineteenth-century Victorian style. The garden (right) complements the mansion's Greek-Revival style while the dining room (below) reflects the elegance of the 1850s. The sterling silver centerpiece was made in London in 1790.

These pages: the Cupples House in St. Louis, Missouri, one of the country's best examples of Richardson Romanesque architecture. The front foyer (below), the southwest sitting room (right) and second-floor Grand Hall (bottom) are all paneled in English oak.

The woodwork in the reception room (left) of Cupples House (these pages) in St. Louis, Missouri, is white mahogany, and the Galeazzo Campi painting of the Nativity is a focal point of the southeast sitting room (below left). The dining room furnishings (bottom) are authentic French Empire, and those in the library (below) are original to the house. The stairway (facing page top) is an adaptation by the architect Thomas B. Annan of an H. H. Richardson design. The pair of matching lamps in the reception room (facing page bottom) are Chinese imports.

The Grand Hallway (left and below) of Cupples House (these pages) contains a nineteenth-century French pier mirror, a commode of the Louis XV-XVI period, and thirteenth-century French Gothic bishop's throne. All the stained glass in the house is the work of Louis Comfort Tiffany, the window on the minstrel's gallery (facing page top) being a particularly fine example. The fireplace in the music room (facing page bottom), one of twenty-two in the house, features an Italian molded-plaster frieze. The clock and candelabra were made in Dresden.

The Phelps House (these pages) in Carthage, Missouri, was designed by its original owner, a local attorney by the name of Colonel William Phelps. The master bedroom (facing page bottom) is one of five. The ladies' parlor (right) features a white marble fireplace set with mosaic tiles. The staircase (below right) provides an alternative to the elevator, one of the first ever installed in a private house. The Phelps family crest may be seen over the library doorway (below).

The Garth Woodside Mansion (facing page) in Hannibal, Missouri, was once the summer home of Colonel John H. Garth, a boyhood friend and neighbor of Mark Twain, whose books may be found in the library (right). The unusual flying staircase of this 1871 house begins in the Grand Hall (below) and spirals up through three stories.

The Garth Woodside Mansion (these pages) houses an impressive collection of Victorian antiques and is open to the public as a bed and breakfast inn. Visitors enjoy a taste of the refined lifestyle of the 1850s.

Rockcliffe Mansion (these pages) in Hannibal, Missouri, was originally the home of lumberman John Cruikshank. Abandoned and empty for forty years, it was known to local children as a haunted house until it was saved from the wreckers and restored in 1967. On his last visit to Hannibal, Mark Twain delivered one of his famous monologues here, from the Grand Staircase (right). The fireplace in the Red Room, or library (below), is one of only two in the house designed to burn wood, all the others being fueled by gas.

The music room (facing page top) of the Rockcliffe Mansion (these pages), lit by imposing Palladian windows, once held two grand pianos. The cabinets above the mahogany fireplace in the dining room (facing page bottom) are set with mirrors to reflect the light from the Tiffany chandelier. The bedrooms (this page) are furnished with original pieces. Each has a private bathroom, the one off Mrs. Cruikshank's room (right) leading to a balcony overlooking the Mississippi River.

These pages: Terrace Hill, in Des Moines, Iowa. Formerly the mansion of businessman Benjamin F. Allen, this 1869 Second Empire structure has been the residence of Iowa's Governor since 1976. The chandelier in the sitting room (facing page bottom and below) is of pierced brass and was made in Turkey; the fireplace is one of eight in the house.

These pages: Salisbury House in Des Moines, Iowa, a copy of King's House in Salisbury, England. The library (facing page bottom) contains an impressive collection of autographs and rare books. The house also contains a valuable collection of artifacts, oriental rugs, tapestries and furniture. The sitting room (below) contains Louis XVI furniture and a portrait of Mrs. Carl Weeks, the wife of the house's original owner, who was a cosmetics manufacturer.

41

Villa Louis (these pages) in Prairie du Chein, Wisconsin, was built in 1868 by the widow of fur trader Hercules Dousman. The light from the stained glass window (right) at the head of the stairway (below) accentuates the richness of the furnishings collected over the years by the family before the house became Wisconsin's first official Historic Site.

Villa Louis (these pages) was named by Nina Dousman, daughter-in-law of Jane Dousman, who had built the house in honor of her late husband. Nina and her five children lived here for two decades, during which time she assembled a collection of fine art and chattels that make the mansion one of the best examples of late-nineteenth-century style anywhere in the country today. Each of the rooms is a frozen moment in time, exactly as Nina Dousman would remember it. Left: Louis' room, (below left) the master bedroom and (below) the parlor. Facing page: (top) the dining room and (bottom) the kitchen.

The Governor's Mansion (these pages and overleaf) in Madison, Wisconsin, was built between 1921 and 1928 as a home for the industrialist Carl Johnson. The state acquired the home, overlooking Lake Mendota, in 1949. The drawing room (facing page bottom) is the main entertaining and living area of the house. The chandelier in the breakfast room (right) is a rare old gas fixture converted to electricity, and the handpainted wallpaper in the dining room (below) features native Wisconsin birds and flowers.

INDEX

The paneling in the gathering room (facing page top) of Fair Lane (these pages) was originally dark stained walnut, but Mrs. Ford had it painted to make the room more cheerful. The mahogany in the dining room (facing page bottom) is richly burnished and the cartouches are carved with wildfowl designs. The master bedroom (below) is the only room furnished with original Ford furniture. The main staircase (bottom) is lit by a 250-year-old Belgian brass chandelier and an English antique stained-glass window.

The home (these pages) of Edsel and Eleanor Ford at Grosse Pointe Shores, Michigan, was built in 1927 to resemble an English Cotswold manor house. The dining room (facing page bottom) contains paneling from an English mansion and was originally lit solely by candlelight. The morning room (top) also contains eighteenth-century English pine paneling. The main hall (above) sets the stage for the warm welcome visitors received during the nearly fifty years the Fords and their four children lived here.

The eighteenth-century French furniture in the drawing room (left) of the Edsel and Eleanor Ford House (these pages) made it a comfortable room for pre-dinner conversation. Family gatherings were usually held around the massive English fireplace in the library (below). The oak stairway (facing page top) was built in 1600 for an English manor house and the oak-paneled study (facing page bottom) has not been altered since Mr. Ford's death in 1943.

The yellow guest bedroom (facing page top) and the master suite of the Ford's house (these pages) at Grosse Pointe Shores, with its comfortable sitting room (facing page bottom) and bedroom (bottom) are furnished with traditional comfort reflecting the design of the house. The children's bedrooms utilize modern Art Deco fixtures (below) and furnishings. Each of the bedroom suites in the house has its own private bathroom.

Spiegel Grove (these pages), the home of President Rutherford B. Hayes in Fremont, Ohio, is furnished with rare Victorian antiques throughout its stately drawing room (facing page bottom and top left), dining room (facing page top right) and intimate parlor (facing page center right), known as the Red Room. Hayes' library (bottom) also served as his office. After his death, the first Presidential library was built on the grounds of the twenty-five-acre estate.

Rutherford B. Hayes' daughter, Fanny, hung a portrait of herself and her famous father in her bedroom (below and facing page top) in Spiegel Grove (these pages). Facing page bottom: the bedroom of Hayes' uncle, Sardis Birchard, who built the house. The master bedroom (bottom) was a private retreat for Hayes and his wife, Lucy. It was one of several rooms they added, doubling the size of the house he inherited during his term as President.

Lawnfield (these pages), the thirty-room Victorian home of President James A. Garfield in Mentor, Ohio, was a rundown farmhouse when he bought it in 1876. The reception room (right) and parlor (below) were refurbished, and no less than twenty-three rooms added. All the furniture in the house today belonged to the Garfield family.

The wide hallway (left) on the second floor of Lawnfield (these pages) was busy during Garfield's 1880 presidential campaign, which was conducted from his study (above). His library (below) contains mementoes of his presidency and the desk he used as a congressman. His wife Lucretia's bedroom (facing page bottom) contains a cradle used for thirty-nine members of the Garfield family, including the President's daughter, Mollie, whose bedroom (facing page top) seems just as she left it.

Sixty-five-room Stan Hywet Hall (these pages) in Akron, Ohio, was built in 1915 as a home for the family of Frank A. Seiberling, a co-founder of Goodyear. The name of the manor house is an adaptation of the Middle English term for "stonehewn" and it is surrounded by seventy acres of gardens and lawns. The Great Hall (facing page) is three stories high and has a medieval timbered ceiling. It is furnished with sixteenth- and seventeenth-century antiques and Flemish tapestries.

The gardens (facing page top and above) of Stan Hywet Hall (these pages) were designed between 1911 and 1915 by Warren Manning and include a teahouse (right) overlooking a lagoon. The music room (facing page bottom) has been called the most beautiful room in America by many interior designers. The walnut-paneled library (below) has Italian designs painted on canvas covering its ceiling.

During holiday celebrations, a Della Robbia-style plaque of the Madonna and Child was hung over the dining room fireplace (left) in Stan Hywet Hall (these pages). The dining room (below) includes an oil on canvas mural of scenes from Chaucer's *Canterbury Tales*, while the breakfast room (facing page top left) displays a collection of antique pewter, glass and pottery. The chandelier and fireplace tiles are delft. The kitchen (facing page top right) has no storage space, having been designed for cooking food to be eaten fresh daily. An *allée* of plane trees (facing page bottom), lined by azaleas and rhododendrons, leads south from the stage of the music room.

148

The Grand Staircase (facing page) of Stan Hywet Hall (these pages) climbs from the basement to the fourth floor tower room. The Emil Fuchs portrait above the stairs is of Mrs. Seiberling and her youngest child, Franklin. At Christmas the Great Hall fireplace is flanked by a yule log (right), an old Seiberling family tradition. Over the fireplace in the solarium (below) a carved panel depicts fruit, foliage, birds and animals. The walls are paneled in sandalwood.

Warren G. Harding ran his campaign for the presidency from the porch of his 1891 home (these pages) in Marion, Ohio. A 1965 restoration returned the dining room (facing page bottom) to its original appearance. Gaslights were also re-installed in the parlor (bottom), Harding's portrait (below left) was flanked by the American and Presidential flags and his desk (below) made ready for another day of work.

Adena (facing page), in Chillicothe, Ohio, is an 1807 Georgian house made of local sandstone for Thomas Worthington, an early governor of Ohio. Its restoration, which includes that of several outbuildings, has returned the hallway (above left), the parlor (above), the dining room (left) and the kitchen (bottom) to their early-nineteenth-century appearance.

Greek-Revival Avery-Downer House (these pages) in Granville, Ohio, dates from 1842 and is now the Robbins Hunter Museum, containing eighteenth- and nineteenth-century antiques and artifacts from all over the world in its fourteen furnished rooms, all open to the public. The chandelier in the ladies' parlor (facing page top) was designed to burn whale oil and the mahogany pianoforte was made in London in the 1790s. A stately grandfather clock graces the dining room (facing page bottom).

The dining room (below) is one of the brightest places in the Avery-Downer House (these pages). The main parlor (bottom) is the most formal, its dark massive Empire furniture representing quality and refinement. The gentlemen's parlor (facing page) includes an 1815 Federal-era three-part mirror over the mantle, which was locally designed to imitate Eastern elegance on the Ohio frontier. The candlesticks were made in Philadelphia in 1840. Overleaf: the reception hall in Avery-Downer House.

Silk wall coverings and a raised French bed dominate Mrs. Wilson's bedroom (above left) at Meadow Brook Hall (these pages). The French bedroom (above) was the Hall's major guest room. A hidden doorway behind the oak paneled walls of Mr. Wilson's study (left) leads to a secret stone stairway. The drawing room (below) contains paintings by Murillo, Turner, Joshua Reynolds and John Constable, while the Chinese Chippendale furniture in the breakfast room (facing page top) is complemented by Oriental decor. The decor of the ballroom (facing page bottom) is informal.

Fair Lane (these pages), in Dearborn, Michigan, was the home of Henry Ford the auto-maker from 1915 until his death in 1947. The oak-paneled library (above) contains 4,000 volumes, including a famous collection of McGuffey Readers. The estate included its own powerhouse (left). The inscription on the cypress beam over the field room fireplace (facing page bottom) is a quotation from Thoreau: "Chop your own wood and it will warm you twice."

These pages: Hearthstone, in Appleton, Wisconsin, the first home to be lit by hydroelectric power. The Edison light switches (below) resemble water faucets, and the light fixtures (below right) are called electroliers. The Eastlake Queen Anne house (bottom) hasn't changed much since 1887, and its Grand Hall (facing page) still welcomes visitors as warmly as it did a century ago.

Parquet floors of Wisconsin hardwood (below) feature in all the rooms in Hearthstone (these pages). Hand carved wood also adorns the house, from the newel post in the front hall (left) to each of the nine ornate fireplaces, including that in the dining room (facing page).

Old Wade House (these pages) in Greenbush, Wisconsin, was built in 1851 as a stagecoach inn at the half way point between Sheboygan and Fond du Lac. The interior, including the parlor (facing page top) and dining room (facing page bottom), was restored in 1953 by the Koehler Foundation and dedicated as a Wisconsin State Park.

All of the twenty-seven rooms in Old Wade House, including guest rooms (facing page top), the parlor (facing page below) and bar room (this page), have been lovingly restored to their appearance when Sylvanus Wade and his wife Betsy welcomed weary travelers at the side of the wooden plank road between the Fox River-Lake Winnebago area and Lake Michigan.

Wingspread (these pages and overleaf), built in 1939 for the H. F. Johnson family in Racine, Wisconsin, is the last and largest of Frank Lloyd Wright's "Prairie Houses." The living areas of the house stand above a raised basement of "Cherokee Red" brick (above). The cantilevered north wing (left) is the only second level. The chimney in the eight-sided living room (facing page) is set with a fireplace on each of its four sides. "We called the house 'Wingspread'," wrote the architect, "because spread its wings it did."

The thirty-foot-high chimney tower is the only emphatically
vertical element in the design of Wingspread (these pages). The
built-in furniture on the main level counteracts its height, and the
mezzanine re-emphasizes the horizontal feeling. The library
contains works detailing Frank Lloyd Wright's other
achievements.

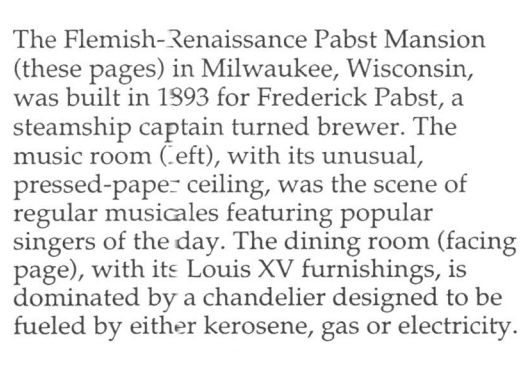

The Flemish-Renaissance Pabst Mansion (these pages) in Milwaukee, Wisconsin, was built in 1893 for Frederick Pabst, a steamship captain turned brewer. The music room (left), with its unusual, pressed-paper ceiling, was the scene of regular musicales featuring popular singers of the day. The dining room (facing page), with its Louis XV furnishings, is dominated by a chandelier designed to be fueled by either kerosene, gas or electricity.

The rococo fireplace in the ladies' parlor (below) of the Pabst Mansion (these pages) sets the tone for the entire room. The folding oak shutters are found throughout the house. Captain

Pabst's Study (facing page top) is a classic German Renaissance room, whilst his grand-daughter's bedroom (facing page bottom) repeats the French rococo theme.

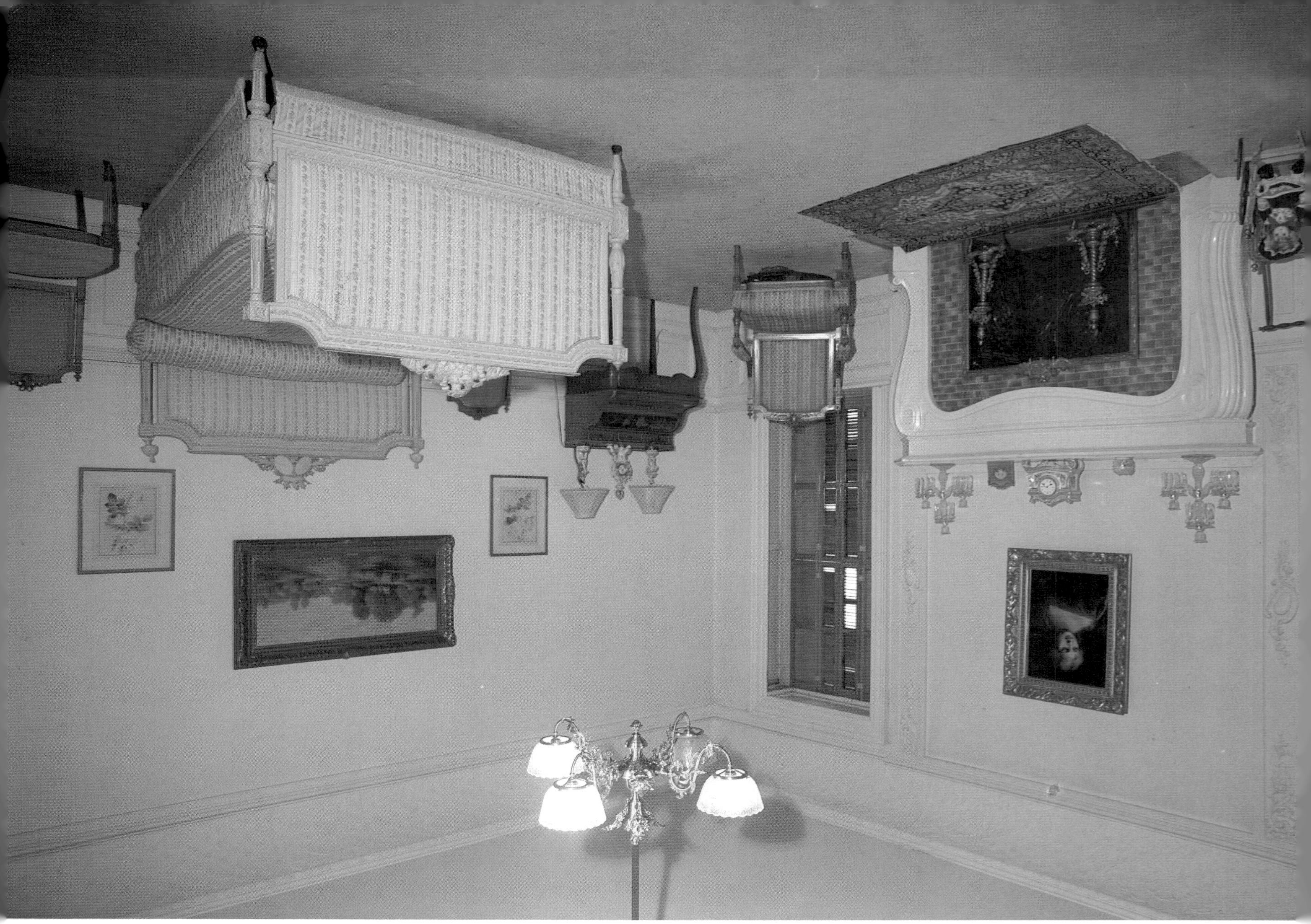

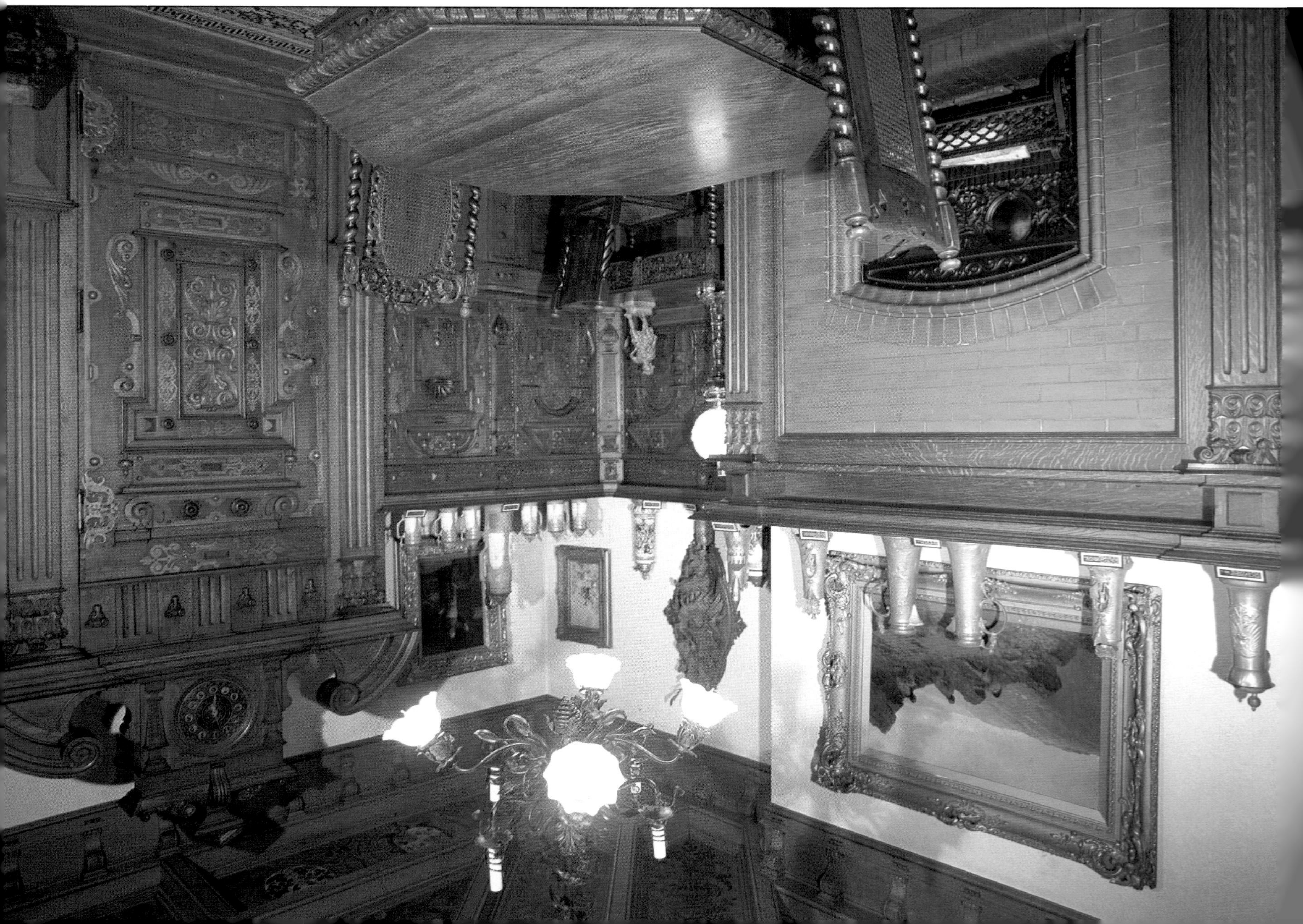

69

The French-Colonial Pierre Menard Home (these pages) in Kaskaskia, Illinois, was built in 1800 by a Candian fur trader who became Illinois' first Lieutenant Governor. The dining room (facing page bottom), hardly adequate for Menard's fourteen children, was the scene of an endless round of parties, making the kitchen (below and bottom right) an unusually active one. The bounty of the kitchen garden (right) kept it well-supplied.

A portrait of Pierre Menard hangs in the parlor (facing page bottom) of his carefully restored house. The master bedroom (facing page top), the nursery (below), and other rooms in the house all reflect the lifestyle of an upper-class family on the frontier in the early eighteenth century.

In 1865 the people of Galena, Illinois, presented an Italianate villa (these pages) to General Ulysses S. Grant. The kitchen (right) contained every modern convenience when the future President moved into the Galena house. The silver service in the dining room (facing page bottom) was later used at the White House. Right: the bedroom used by General Grant's daughter, Nellie, heated by a small boiler. When he was at home here, Grant conducted his business in the library (bottom right), which contains a small sculpture, *Council of War*, (below) representing General Grant, President Lincoln and Secretary of War Edwin Stanton.

Ronald Reagan's boyhood home (these pages) in Dixon, Illinois, has been restored to its appearance in the years of the Depression, when the former President lived there. The dining room (left) is set for four, as it would have been then, and the bedroom (below left) that Ronald shared with his brother contains mementoes of his boyhood. The kitchen (bottom left) still holds the old icebox the boys kept filled with water, and the bathroom (below) is still supplied with the razor strop their father used to keep them on the straight and narrow.

The 1837 Henry B. Clarke House (these pages), the oldest house in Chicago, has been moved twice, most recently in 1977 to South Indiana Avenue. The rooms in this Greek-Revival house, including the southwest parlor (below), have been furnished as they would have been in the 1840s and '50s.

All the rooms in the Clarke House, including the master bedroom (facing page top), southwest parlor (facing page bottom), the dining room (below) and the music room (bottom) were furnished with authentic pieces. The work was carried out by the National Society of Colonial Dames of America in the State of Illinois. Their consultant, Robert A. Furhoff, supervised the recreation of the interiors, including that of the hallways and landings (right).

These pages: the 1886 John J. Glessner House on Prairie Avenue in Chicago, the city's only surviving building by Henry Hobson Richardson, and the only Richardson house in the country open to the public. The Glessners lived in the house for more than four decades, during which time the butler's pantry (facing page top) and the kitchen (facing page bottom) would have been full of activity.

The entrance hall (facing page top) of Glessner House (these pages) was inspired by that of a 16th-century English country house. The schoolroom (facing page bottom) has small windows, reflecting the architect's belief that front windows in urban houses are not for looking out of. The library windows not facing the street (right), like those of the master bedroom (below), are more generously proportioned.

The Glessner House's granite exterior gives way to brick in its inner courtyard (below), a fact that allowed an innovative floor plan. The dining room (facing page top) and the parlor (facing page bottom), both facing the courtyard, have details and furnishings specified by Richardson himself.

The 1872 Victorian mansion (above) of U.S. Supreme Court Justice David Davis, in Bloomington, Illinois, was designed by Alfred Picquenard in an imaginative combination of architectural styles. The interior (facing page) is decorated and furnished to the height of Victorian fashion. Only the sitting room (bottom left) could be called at all "casual," containing such furnishings as the Judge's maple rocking chair.

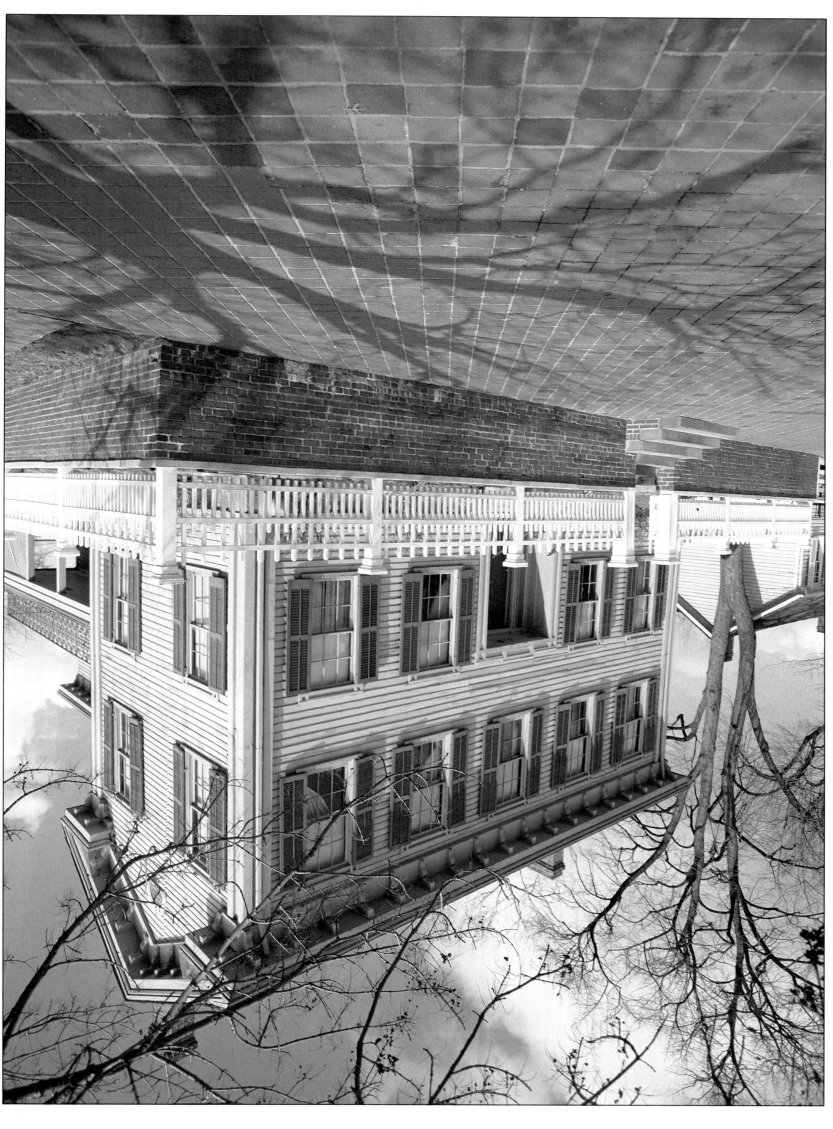

Though Abraham Lincoln was born in a log cabin, his career as a lawyer in Springfield, Illinois, enabled him to buy a fine Greek-Revival frame house (these pages). The house was roomy enough for the Lincolns to boast a guest room (facing page top), but their four sons bunked together in another room (facing page bottom).

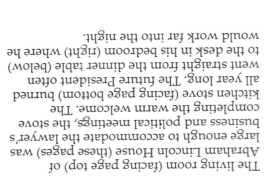

The living room (facing page top) of Abraham Lincoln House (these pages) was large enough to accommodate the lawyer's business and political meetings, the stove completing the warm welcome. The kitchen stove (facing page bottom) burned all year long. The future President often went straight from the dinner table (below) to the desk in his bedroom (right) where he would work far into the night.

These pages: Copshaholm, the 1897 Queen Anne home of industrialist Joseph D. Oliver in South Bend, Indiana. It was designed by Charles A. Rich, who also created Theodore Roosevelt's Sagamore Hill near New York City. The rich interior, from the Great Hall (above) to the landing on the Grand Stairway (left), the sitting room (facing page top), and dining room (facing page bottom) reflect elegant nineteenth-century comfort.

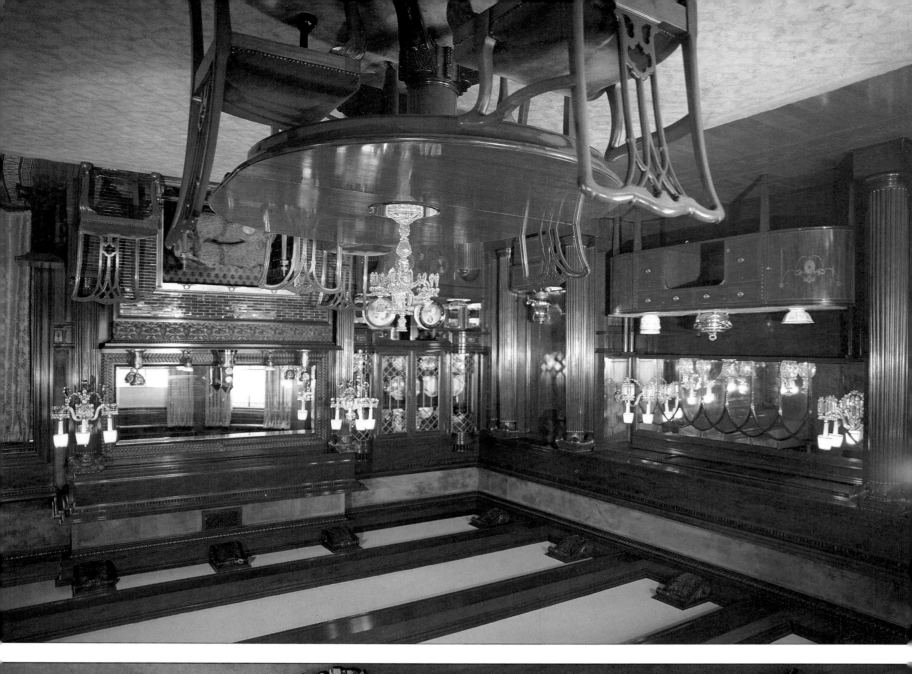

The Olivers' bedroom (facing page top), like all the bedrooms in Copshaholm (these pages), was designed to be a private, quiet sanctuary. One of the guest rooms was reserved for Mrs. Oliver's mother, and is known as Grandmother Wells' Room (facing page bottom). Right: the music room seen through wrought-iron grillwork from the central hallway. Its four-foot-high stone frieze (below right), representing Greek musicians, is a copy of an original by Lucca Della Robbia. Mr. Oliver's den (below), with its high, vaulted ceiling, is paneled in oak and includes a fireplace ten feet wide. The French-inspired, feminine morning room (bottom right) was also used as a reception room.

Financier James Lanier built a magnificent Greek-Revival mansion (these pages) on the banks of the Ohio River in Madison, Indiana, in 1844. The work of architect Francis Costigan, it ranks among the grandest of the grand homes of the South. The Sheraton-furnished dining room (facing page top left) is lit by one of the first gaslight chandeliers in Indiana. The ceiling of the entrance hall (facing page top, right) is decorated in gold leaf. The double parlors (facing page bottom) can be separated by concealed doors.

The portrait over the desk in the study (facing page top) of Lanier House (these pages) is of James Lanier's first wife, Elizabeth. The financier's second wife, Mary, is represented in the portrait in the parlor (facing page bottom), which is still furnished with a mirror and chandelier original to the house. Mrs. Lanier's bedroom (right) contains a trundle bed. James' two sons by his first wife shared the bedroom (below) at the northwest corner of the house. Elizabeth was the mother of six and Mary had three children.

Except for his four years as the twenty-third President of the United States and six years in the U.S. Senate, a sixteen-room mansion (these pages) in Indianapolis was the home of Benjamin Harrison from its construction in 1875 until his death in 1901. When the house was modernized in 1897 the original furniture from the nursery (left) and the dining room (facing page top) was stored in the ballroom, which helped make restoring the house to its original appearance relatively easy. The library (facing page bottom) also contains furniture that was in the room when Harrison planned his presidential campaign.

The master (facing page top left) and guest bedrooms (facing page top right) of the Benjamin Harrison House (these pages) have been restored to their original appearance. President Harrison's portrait has been added over the fireplace in the back parlor (right), and the studio (facing page bottom) that his wife Carrie used, is filled with her own creations. The front parlor (below) reflects the formal elegance of the 1875 era, when Harrison built the house for just $21,130.10.

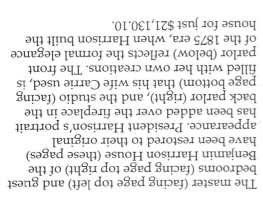

The Morris-Butler House (these pages), a Second Empire Italianate villa in Indianapolis, Indiana, was built in 1864. The Queen Anne porch (below) was added in 1882. It is now a museum used as a learning center for architectural and historical preservation. The parlor (right) is an example of high style rococo revival. The hallway (bottom) sets the stage for the house's collection of Victoriana.

The Morris Butler House (these pages), Indianapolis, Indiana, contains some important pieces, including the Wooten desk in Noble Butler's office (left), an example of "industrial style" that was made in the town. The library (below) could provide extra space for large dinner parties if the doors connecting it with the dining room beyond were opened. The decorations in the dining room (facing page top) itself are all references to food, following a typically Victorian fashion. The morning room (facing page bottom) was used as a family room and for informal entertaining.

Future President William Henry Harrison built his house (these pages) at Vincennes, Indiana, in 1804 after he was made Governor of the territory. The dining room (facing page bottom), kitchen (right) and parlor (below right) all bustled with activity as Harrison conducted his official business in the house. The bedrooms (bottom pictures) provided him and his family with quiet privacy. The hallway (below), like all the rooms in the house, is much larger than it appears as Harrison wanted to create a sense of intimacy in the home he called "Grouseland," itself a copy of the Virginia plantation house where he was born.

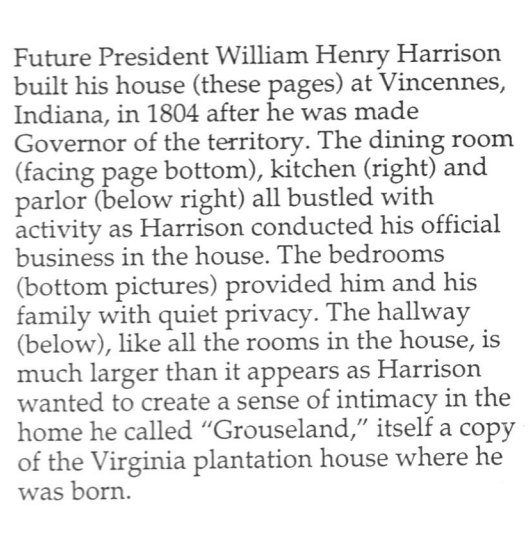

Hillforest (these pages) was built in 1856 in Aurora, Indiana, by industrialist and financier Thomas Gaff. It has a rounded façade made to resemble a steamboat, one of the sources of Gaff's wealth. The suspended staircase (left) imitates those in riverboat salons. The twin parlors (facing page) have been carefully restored to their original appearance and the dining room (below) retains the intimacy the Gaffs treasured.

These pages: Honolulu House in Marshall, Michigan, built in 1860 for Judge Abner Pratt, who had served as U.S. Consul to the Hawaiian Islands. It is a combination of Italianate, Gothic and Polynesian architecture. The dining room (below) honors the Marshall Historical Society's Anne J. Ells, who retrieved its furniture from the state archives.

The family parlor (facing page top) of Honolulu House (these pages) contains portraits of George and Sidney Ketchum, the founders of Marshall. The twin fireplaces are of slate painted to look like marble. The elaborate ceiling in the formal parlor (facing page bottom) picks up the pattern of the carpet, which was designed for the house. Right: the stairway curving up from the center of the hallway. The dining room furniture (below) was exhibited at Philadelphia's Centennial Exposition in 1876.

The Neo-Classical Abbie and Genevieve Schoenberger House (these pages) in Ludington, Michigan, was built in 1903 for Warren Cartier, a local lumberman. He lavished it with fine woods, such as the oak in the main hallway (below) and stairway (right), and black cherry in the living room (above). He built its imposing second-floor balcony (facing page) to be the setting for his acceptance speech as Governor of Michigan, but the voters denied him the opportunity of using it.

Genevieve Schoenberger's bedroom (facing page top) is an oasis of light femininity; most of the Schoenberger House (these pages) is filled with dark woods such as the American sycamore in the living room dining room (facing page bottom). The floors in the living room

and dining room (below) are exquisitely detailed, as is all the fine woodwork in the house, which is maintained as a private residence.

Hundred-room, Tudor-style Meadow Brook Hall (these pages) in Rochester, Michigan, was built in 1926 by Matilda Wilson and her husband. Mrs Wilson was the widow of John Dodge, the automobile pioneer, and she had the house designed by William E. Kapp. The wood-ribbed ceiling in the main gallery (facing page bottom) and the beamed ceiling of the ballroom (below) are modeled on English originals. The ceiling of the sun room (overleaf) resembles that of an English chapel, and its arched windows look out over a traditionally English garden.